1

AGENTS

Help productivity.

Graeme Smith

PUBLISHED ON AMAZON.com
by
LABYRINTH BOOKS

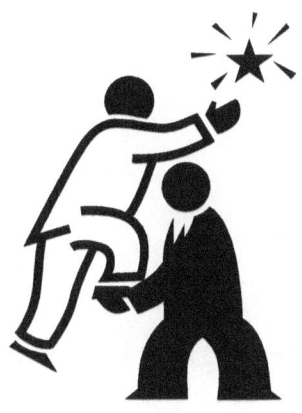

DEDICATION:

This book is dedicated to my family.

    Hele-ly (Ly).
          my wife:

    Ingrid.
          our daughter:

    Marie.
          my former wife:

    Fiona, Natalie and Michael
          our children:

    Georgie
          Michael's wife:

    Pearl, Kiki and Martha.
          their children:

They have had to put up with me for many years and I thank them for that.
I hope this book gives them an insight into what has occupied me.
All have done worthwhile and interesting things in the absence of my help.
I congratulate them for their achievements.

THANKS:

I greatly appreciate the contribution made to this book by comments and suggestions from:

Mike Barr – Adelaide, Australia

Richard Bruland - Los Angeles, USA

Tracey Creighton - Merimbula, Australia

Evelyn Dunphy – Maine, USA

Geoff Fellows – Wagga Wagga, Australia

Michelle Grace - Brisbane, Australia

Leanne Halls – North Sydney, Australia

Heidi Jeffries – Ferny Hills, Australia

Kathy Kay Voysey - Mudgee, Australia.

Vince Miller - 'Australian Artist' / 'International Artist

John Newell - Ontario, Canada

David Voigt – Yarramalong, Australia.

HOW TO USE THIS BOOK.

First think - then do.
Usually people don't think through things to the level they need to.
Because of that, they have projects instead of tasks on their "to do" list.
That leads to procrastination as it hasn't been broken down to a task level.

So go through your book once to understand it.
Go through it again.

Then start at the idea you would like to implement first.
Make notes of the steps you will need to take and the resources required.
Use these notes to create a step by step system for implementing the guide.
Often you will not refer to the original, once you've created **YOUR** system.

The first question to ask and answer is "Why is this being done?"
How does this align with where you want to get to?
What are the strategic implications of doing this?
Does this fit with getting to your goal in the shortest and fastest time?
What would it be like if it were totally successful?
Define it - what is success for this project and how will you know?

Now brainstorm all the tasks that are involved in your project.
It's important not to go linear too fast with this.
By linear, I mean step one, step two, step three, and step four.
You end up cutting off options.
As you plan step one, two, three, there is a specific step that might be four.
Start steps too quickly, other ways for one, two and three may not appear.

The first third of any brainstorming session is really easy.
Just come up with lots of ideas.
The second third is challenging - go through ideas and see where they lead.
Then push yourself to think a little bit outside the box.
That's often where the big idea is!
That's where the most powerful way of getting a project done fastest - is.

Most people never get to that level and short-change themselves.
Then their project takes longer and they also set up to procrastinate.
This final brainstorming part of the equation is incredibly important.

Once fully brainstormed put your options into a linear sequence.
Then you can figure out what you've overlooked.
Everything becomes obvious as you get your tasks in order.
Now add missing steps and you have laid out your task list for this project.

Decide what things can you start immediately?
What can be started that are not dependent on what occurred before them?
Obviously that is step one.
There might be step five, six or twenty that don't rely on anything else to do.
You can get started on them right away too.

Now use a folder.
Write things you think of at the time and also cross off things as you do them.
Add in stuff that is relevant from time to time.

WHAT IS MARKETING?

Marketing is the process of finding buyers AND making sales
It is exactly the same process no matter what is being sold!
In some cases the process is simple like selling apples at a roadside stall.
It can be very complex like selling aero-planes for a government's air-force.
Most, including selling artworks, is somewhere in between these poles.

Think about fishing and you'll understand marketing.
Does a fisherman catch fish in a desert when there are simply no fish there.

You must market where there are possible buyers.
A fisherman must go where the fish are – where there is water.
That's a start but there are still no fish in a swimming pool are there?
They need to be in the right kind of water – a river, lake or at sea.

But different fish swim in different waters!
Sharks and marlin are in the ocean, while bream live mainly in rivers.
Likewise you must know who you are targeting with your marketing.
Will it be businesses, first home buyers, investors or what?
Each will need a different marketing program.

OK you are now in the right water for the kind of fish you are after!
Some species are nocturnal and they will not be caught during the day.
Your marketing needs to be when the target is likely to be most receptive.
Will it be at work, nights or weekends?

You are at the right place and time so how do you catch the fish?
Usually you'll have a fishing rod.
Is it the right kind for the fish you want to catch?
You won't catch a shark with the kind of rod that takes a trout!
Your marketing must be attractive to the people you are after.

Do you have the right bait?
Again different bait attracts different fish.

A carcass for the shark but just a worm for many other species.
Can you provide something that your target market will find attractive?

But throwing any bait into the water catches nothing at all!
The bait must be attached to a hook.
Without the fish taking the hook there is no catch.
Different hooks are needed for different kinds of fish.

Different hooks are also needed for different markets.
The right hook gets your market to take the next step to a purchase.
But this only needs to be a little step.

But hooks only catch the fish.
They're in the water, not your boat or beach, a hook is on the end of a line.
Is your line strong enough you the fish you are after?
Again this varies for the kind of fish.
How do you get your prospect to seriously consider what you sell?
For someone buying a print it will not need to be sophisticated.
But selling an original Renoir will be considerably more complicated.

That still no fish for the line has to have a reel for that to happen.
Again different reels for different fish.
The right reel allows you to bring the fish to the end of your fishing line.
But it's still not in the boat is it?

You must lift the fish out of the water into your boat or onto the beach.
Fishing nets do this so now you have your catch.
The fish is yours to do what you want with.

You can even sell the fish but who might want to buy?
It could be someone who sells fish for food or live for a fish-tank or pool.
They could even be for re-stocking natural water places.

Where can you find them?
You must look where the fish buyers are!

Follow the path of the fisherman.
And eventually you have a prospect asking can they buy.
You have made a sale AND you can make more sales the same way.

Making the sale is a five step process.
In order you work from the top through to the bottom group.

      SUSPECTS are people who possibly want what you have for sale.

      PROSPECTS are people likely to want what you have for sale.

      BUYERS are those who have bought what you are selling.

      REPEAT BUYERS continue to buy what you sell.

      ADVOCATES help you sell to others.

The reverse sequence is the order of importance to your sales.

INDEX: AGENTS HELP PRODUCTIVITY

Chapter One: Your career vision.   14
Chapter Two: Could an agent help?   22
Chapter Three: Find an agent.   28

WHERE NEXT?   **48**
NOT NOW: **49**
SEND TO: **50**

Chapter One: Your career vision.

1. Do you have a long term vision about your career?
2. Is there a magic bullet?
3. A professional artist is not merely a painter - that is an artist.
4. What advantage is there if you have your own agent?
5. The start stops most people.

1. Do you have a long term vision about your career?

Most artists tend to focus on an individual painting.
An exhibition is a collection of their paintings.
But what if the focus is on the exhibition, as one of a series of exhibitions?
Then there's a different mind-set.

A career can be an ongoing stream of exhibitions.
You can generate this income stream if you know what to do.
A successful artist should have this knowledge.

But even if you do you might not have the available time!
You don't need to do it but someone does!
A key element is people willing to buy your work.

You need sales and marketing a major gallery provides its main artists.
This is essential BUT someone has to do it.

There's a lot of day to day stuff that needs doing in any profession.
An artist is no different and the more successful you are the more there is.
Meet people, phone calls, enter competitions, framing, finances, etc.
So where do you get the time from?

You'll have to do all this yourself initially.
Eventually you need an agent and you'll know exactly why you want them.
Instead of the agent telling you what they want.

2. Is there a magic bullet?

There is NO way art business becomes a successful career overnight.
You just can't skip the fundamental steps needed for a solid business.
Well, I have some news for you which should be encouraging.
It **IS** possible to build a money-making art career without breaking the bank.

But you've got to do things right the first time!
In terms of finding your own agent that is the focus of this Focus.
Then your career path will open up for you.

But there ARE wrong ways.
If you try to cut corners, it means *10 times the work* in the long run.
So you've got to be patient!
Even if you do things right, you can't do them all concurrently.
That means there is no short cut to success.

Once something is learned it can be built in ways not possible before.
But you have to start with that initial learning.
Then relatively small ideas can become altered and improved.

Most people have heard of the downward spiral or vicious circle.
The poor get poorer, have more children, lose jobs or can't get a job.
Everything seems to continually get worse.

On the other hand there is an upward spiral too.
Things start in a small, insignificant way and gradually increase momentum.
This happens as they link with an increasing number of other ideas.
This upwards spiral is integral to the creative process.
It also provides the momentum leading to success.

So while there is no short cut there's a spiral you can climb aboard.
That happens if you focus on maintaining momentum not get to the end.
Even with small steps the former attitude will lead to the latter attainment.

Spirals can be powerful.

They seem to fuel themselves and become self-propelling in time.

Successful people get more opportunities to be even more successful.

Those who need opportunities never seem to get even one!

Many people think this is luck, either good or bad depending on its nature.

But we make our own luck.

Good ideas can come from anywhere.

It's up to you to notice and be open to them.

You also need to harness them to your advantage.

They can be painting ideas, but career ideas are subject to the same force.

This momentum can accompany a career as it is rejuvenated too.

Change will build slowly at first but gradually gain momentum.

Other spirals interlock and momentum gathers more rapidly.

In time success is attained once more.

3. A professional artist is not merely a painter - that is an artist.

You are also in business, have a career, or are in a profession.
Money is a measure of how well you do.
It's not the motivation, that's your desire to follow your dream.
But money does say something about how well you've followed the dream.
It also makes achieving your dream more feasible.

It's likely more income leads to a better lifestyle but not better work.
You can live in a garret in poverty or have whatever lifestyle you'd like.
Either way your work will remain of much the same standard.
Often artists assume the artwork sells itself - people fall in love with the work.
Marketing is a matter of putting people in front of paintings (an exhibition).

An exhibition sells none or a few works they were NOT 'good'.
This explanation is widely accepted.
Artists, galleries or other exhibition organizers and potential buyers all agree.
But what if you have done your best, as is usually the case?
What can you do if in with this situation other than change what you paint?
It seems very little.

BUT what if the assumption itself was questioned instead?
In other words artworks do NOT sell themselves.
Then one has to speculate on what does sell and why do people buy them?
This is a more productive line of thinking.
Let's consider a well-known example of a failed artist.

Were all those paintings that van Gogh did substandard?
They didn't sell whilst he was alive and now they bring astronomical prices.
Have they changed since?
BUT the paintings are still the same as the day they were done.
If they were "bad" in Vincent's day you would suppose they are still "bad".

What HAS changed is people's opinion rather than the works.
Opinion is something that astute marketing can and should influence.

That's one of the roles of marketing.
Instead of blaming your painting for a failure to sell question the marketing.
Was there a failure to influence people's opinion in relation to your paintings?
Possibly there was a failure to find out what opinions were held to start with?

You have to earn money so you need to master the art of marketing!
Most artists think very little about marketing.
They hand it over to someone else hoping they know what to do.
But many of those people do NOT know what to do.
Most people do not have a clue about most things they buy!
When you shop for anything how specific is your 'decision-making' criteria?
How expert are you in areas like law, bedding, accountancy, or real estate?
Probably not much of an expert at all!
And therein is an extraordinary opportunity.

Most of your potential buyers don't have sophisticated buying criteria.
They have an idea what the prospective purchase could do for them.
They might even know what they paid in the past and that's about it!

That means you can re-set the buying criteria for your entire market.
Most people come to most buying situations with flexible buying criteria.
Can you make your works their most logical choice?
And at the same time provide the best financial result for you.
All this without changing what you paint!

4. What advantage is there if you have your own agent?

A lot of day to day stuff needs doing in any profession, including artist.
The more successful you are the more of it there is.
Meet people, phone calls, enter competitions, framing, handle finances, etc.
Where do you get the time from?

The more successful you are the more you need an agent.
Then you can spend more time painting when you have an agent!
If you've sold works yourself, you'll know what you want your agent to do.
Otherwise the agent will tell you what THEY want!

BUT your agent can do other things you don't do.
An agent can follow people up.
Publicity is worth the effort and your agent can generate it.
That way an agent can harness your reservoir of good will.
Your agent can promote you in ways that you can't do easily.
Using your contact list your agent will leverage sales opportunities too.

Through your agent you will have more control of the selling process.
Your agent presents works for people to buy!
The agent influences others and sell your art on your behalf.
You will be able to work more effectively with a gallery.
Your agent will even help you find the right gallery.

Using your agent you'll find the best way to approach a gallery.
Finalizing the gallery deal will lead to better arrangements for you.
Your agent can supplement the gallery's selling strategies.
Your agent will make a successful exhibition more likely too.
Successful exhibitions are not a myth.
Successful exhibitions have well-defined characteristics.
Your agent can work well within this framework.

5. The start stops most people.

Back in my art student days I learnt how to deal with this problem.
I was in the third year of a four-year art course.
One memorable evening I arrived for class to find I was the only person there!
I wasn't happy but decided not to waste my time.

I looked at my blank canvas and didn't know what to do.
Yes the start certainly had me stopped.

Have you had this feeling?
If I was going to waste some paint it may as well be a colour I didn't like!

I didn't know what to do though.
So I mixed Indian red with some turps, still with no real idea about what to do.
Then just because the paint was runny, I flicked some onto the canvas.
I splashed some more.
Still further splashes followed the first ones.
It was a bit like an Indian red "Jackson Pollock".

Still not knowing what to do, I decided to join up the dots.
I was pleased with the result which I had not anticipated before starting.

The next week the same thing happened.
This time I shut my eyes and made random marks.

But no longer did the start stop me.
I had found out the solution to that particular artistic problem.
It doesn't matter what you do at the start, as long as you do something.
It can even be random although that doesn't necessarily have to be the case.

Getting an agent is no different!
Don't wait, just get on with it and find one.
Just get started looking and your imagination can work for you!
What will you want your agent to do when you find one?

Chapter Two: Could an agent help?

1. Having money is the best way to save time.
2. An agent can help you sell more effectively.

1. Having money is the best way to save time.

Money means you can pay people to do whatever you want.
You only have to do whatever you want to do.
Your time is under your control.
That's why you are a professional artist.
That's also why you have an agent.
If you are successful you only need to paint, and maybe not even that.

Break down large jobs into manageable chunks.
Perhaps you've only got 30 minutes to spare?
How can you accomplish a chore that's going to take days to complete?
Easy – get your agent on the job.

Just take it one small step at a time.
Instead of being overwhelmed break it into smaller, easily manageable bits.
You'll be surprised how much you can accomplish in 30 minutes if you **DO** it.

You'll be even more surprised at how much your agent can do.
Create a schedule of clear and achievable tasks for you to do every day.
Do what you must to make sure you complete each daily task on your list.
Don't go to bed until it's done.
Your agent should also have their schedule.

A professional artist is a self-employed business person.
It's impossible to be successful at business without paying ahead of earning.
An artist is no different.
This still applies when you have an agent!

In the beginning you pay your costs or have an independent income.
So you will also need to keep your spending under tight control!
There will be better returns as time rolls by!
The amounts are hypothetical but illustrate financial considerations:
Let's say your agent sets up a sell-out exhibition each year – just one.
Initial investment is framing, printing, photography, gallery commission.

Initial investment = $
Plus first agent initiated promotion = $10000 (including gallery commission)
Total cost first agent initiated promotion about $10000 + $.
Cost of other agent initiated promotion = $500 (and gallery commission)
Cost of subsequent agent initiated promotions = $2500

Your budget might look like this:

Time	Money earned	Money made
1 year	- $	- $ (you are painting)
2 years	$10000	$10000+$ - $10000+$ = $nil
3 years	$7500	$7500 - $2500 = $5000
4 years	$15000	$15000 - $4500 + $5000 = $15500

Income in years 3 and 4 is net, after paying your agent.

Each agent initiated promotion will build on those that went before.
At some point your prices WILL move past your present levels.
Costs are less as other activity picks up more and some is no longer needed.
In future years your prices can increase dramatically!
Referrals increase the number of works you can sell too.

OK these amounts may not be exactly what you will earn.
BUT they do provide an idea of the kind of thing that is possible.
They do not guarantee anyone will achieve the same or similar results.
As with any business, your results may vary but will be based on:
Background, dedication, motivation, business experience, expertise, desire.

There is no cost-free way to employ your own agent!
Usually your works must be sold to earn money.

Thus a break-even promotion would be very satisfactory to start with.
It can set up your future.
Eventually your agent must develop non-sales income to add to extra sales.

2. An agent can help you sell more effectively if they understand buyers.

Buyers have money to buy paintings.
Understand that good paintings have monetary value.
Like to look at paintings and get something from the experience.
Like to own things they like to look at (collector).

So the buyer needs to spend time with the painting.
Like to display things they own and have a place to do so.
Want to be admired and understood for things they own and collect.
Their collection is their art as it communicates about them.

Most buyers are middle-aged to elderly.
They've well-established careers where they are active or comfortably retired.
Had parents who valued and/or collected paintings etc.
Their children often inherit collections but also the drive as well.
Are probably well educated.
Their collection could be an aspect of their on-going education.
Read books and have them around.
Support other arts.
Don't waste your time on anyone else – they want to monopolize your time.

Try these tests?
Do they want to look at the painting or hear you talk?
When they are looking do they really see the work or talk (can't do both)?
When looking, are they reminded of a relative who paints?

Ask the prospect to take it closer to the natural light.
Tell the prospect to lean the work against the wall and step back for a look.
How was it placed down?
The prospect should treat the work as if it is a car bomb.
But you and your agent know art is a business!

I have given quite a few of my car portraits away.
I am developing a market for these because at the moment there is none.

I also thought there would be a market for prints (and there is).
But here they should be less specific, so they could be everyone's car.
I started a couple of paintings destined to become such prints.
They still haven't been finished.
I've become involved helping artists with their careers rather than my own.

But let's say I do get those prints done!
Then I'll have a lot of stuff to sell – that's the nature of publishing prints!

But first I need to know who the print buying prospects and clients are!
The contact list for my car paintings is likely to be quite specialized!
Generally it will be owners of such cars as I paint.
It will also be their family who might want a gift for the owner.
It could be overseas people too.
I have details of car clubs which can provide the people I need to reach.

Say I want to sell many prints, quickly.
This is easier if the print run is 20 than if it is 500.

The key to successful marketing of prints is NOT to publish too many.
It's also in having all hands on deck selling (agent and gallery).
No matter what printing method is chosen, each is a copy of your original.
You are not producing an artwork, but a print to be sold cheaply in multiples.
Use this knowledge to make a print from one of your paintings is a next step.

There are alternatives to traditional printing process worth considering.
Giclee is more flexible than traditional methods particularly for small editions.
This process offers these advantages at a higher price but better quality.

BUT other alternatives are even cheaper.
Coloured reproductions on a photocopier are probably the cheapest of all.
Produce a print yourself, on a computer instead of professionally worthwhile.
The cost is low and you only need to print the exact number you can sell.

Framed, one print looks the same as any other, no matter how done.
If your print is on quality paper, then you might be able to get a higher price.

But one of the main reasons people buy prints is the low cost.
If enough people like your images producing prints is feasible.
It's also quite likely these people will like more than one of your works.
So they can become future buyers, provided you know who they are.

With horse racing, race clubs, owners, jockeys, trainers, are the focus.
Your agent could be better at penetrating this market than a gallery.
Annual print linked with major events (Melbourne Cup, Kentucky Derby).
Other times would be suitable (maybe Father's Day instead of Mother's Day).
It doesn't matter how many other artists paint horses.
You are not out there competing with them.

The number printed in an edition is a marketing choice.
You can enhance the idea of greater value because of the limited production.
Supply certificates of authenticity and other promotional material.

Then you can also ask higher prices.
But don't.
I would provide certificates etc. now.
Leave the higher prices for down the track a little.
Make sure your agent or gallery get the name and address of each buyer.
This is very important for these people are potential buyers of more prints.
So, next year, they can be contacted early by mail or email.

Chapter Three: Find an agent.

1. What sort of person are you?
2. What is your ideal agent like?
3. You are not looking for a sales person.
4. An agent is a solution to your problems.
5. Here's one way to find an agent!
6. Can you train someone to work for you?
7. More money = better work?
8. A commission base for your agent.

1. What sort of person are you?

A serious commitment to employ an agent requires honest assessment.
What do you want to achieve by employing an agent?
What do you have to do to get that and are you prepared to pay the price?
Agents are for sports, actors, authors, models, musicians and media people.
The agent and people they represent, make considerable sums of money.
Not long ago their clients were in the same position artists these days.
So there's a great opportunity for such a profession to grow.

Lawyers and accountants are backgrounds from which agents come.
They have expertise in negotiating, drawing up contracts, finance and so on.
They are not usually former elite sports players for example.

There are few agents around in spite of a strong demand from artists.
Portrait brokers work somewhat like art agents.
There are 3 or 4 big firms in USA, I'm aware of, and several smaller ones.
They have a large sales staff (like up to 75) spread out around the country.
They are usually women who work strictly on commission.
They throw parties and introduce people to artists and their work.

All the brokerage houses handle most of the major portrait artists.
Check out the Internet and you'll probably find them.
Make an appointment and see if they like your work.
A consensus of their main people decide if they think they can sell you or not.

Let's say you are a portrait painter.
Study hard, spend some on a portfolio and hope a brokerage will take you.
But the odds aren't good.
One broker had 250 portfolios submitted one year and took one new artist.
There were two the year before.
They like to keep all their people so are careful not to be flooded with talent.

Art galleries are often agents for their artists too.
Such galleries prefer to take on an established artist who interests them.
They're selective and difficult to identify, particularly for unestablished artists.

So why does there seem to be so few agents around?
If they can't sell your works they'll be looking for another job.
They favour artists who are established, high priced, and make them money.
They must do this as there is no choice without another source of income.

As an artist you are in a similar position.
You have to sell, if not to the final buyer, then to the gallery or agent.
This involves a great deal of work so you have to put your business hat on.
You can invite someone to your studio or view a website (virtual studio).
You could show a portfolio with slides.

But there IS a key to this whole issue!
Making money is a problem for an artist and it's also a problem for the agent.
A more experienced artist also seeks to save time (as they know what to do).
A less experienced artist a financial return they can't get with their own effort.
In business money is the driver as failure to make money is out of business.

All art professionals (agents, gallery people) want to make money.
If they can sell enough, or the prices are high enough they are interested.
Your main thrust has to be how they can make money by selling your art.

Solve their problem and they'll solve yours!
So you need to think about how they can make money by selling your art.
How you can help them do this AND how much might they actually get?
You won't abandon your artistic integrity if you adopt a commercial approach.

That finished when you completed the painting.
You WILL adopt a professional attitude which you MUST for an art career.
Prove to them, your work can be marketed, and your chances improve.

One artist said his agent did a great deal and was worth every penny.
He sold, organized promotion, billed, collected, kept books, paid 25 % costs.
But an agent may not be the answer to every artist's prayer.
Having one can be even worse than not having an agent.
Agents cheat, lie, overcharge, delay payment, don't pay at all, swindle, steal.
They invest your money for their benefit, in any way they can take you down.
In this case the artist is referring to agents who also run galleries.

Even without that view there are still potential problems.
Handling stock and organizing deliveries takes time, effort and expense.
The cost to send framed work across USA, Canada or Australia is significant.
They're all big countries so who pays?

YOU have to show commitment to expect it in return.
They put time, money and effort into promoting you to build your reputation.
They'll want you to be around long enough for that investment to pay off.
If you are well known much of this won't need to be done, it has taken place.
It has taken place by word of mouth, others have done your job for you.

Say you've done well so far and are set to meet a prospective agent.
Are you easy to work with, in business there's no room for temperament?
BUT what will they want to know?
Whatever career stage you are at they'll ask why you want to be successful.
Wanting to make money, in this environment, is an acceptable answer.

This is the kind of stuff a prospective agent needs to know.
What do you think the market for your artwork is?
Who has bought your work and are they particular types of people?
Why do they buy it and how much do they pay?
Are there certain venues where your work seems to sell well?

It will help them do their job better, which is what you want.
Do they sell in your normal price range or a little higher?
They may want to know what you believe your USP is.
What is unique about you or your art that separates it from other people?
Tell them about past exhibitions and how well your works sold.
It is desirable to give references to buyers if the buyer doesn't mind.

They will need to know about your production.
How many works do you have for sale right now?
How many do you do in a year?
What sizes are they?
What is your typical price range?

How long does it take to produce (say) ten works?
Your agent or gallery will need a stock of works or they can't really do much.
Be realistic about what you can supply, not optimistic.
There must be a good rapport between the artist and agent.
That will allow open and frank feedback from both sides.

Credible accounting systems are essential, particularly by the agent.
This will go a long way to exposing dishonesty, like work x was sold for $400.
If the price was actually $500.
Such behaviour should not be tolerated at all.

There must be an agreement about how money earned is apportioned.
Know exactly what the financial structure is before you get involved.
You should determine your position in order to negotiate a fair fee.
Decide whether you can cope with the pricing aspect and still make a profit.
An unknown artist cannot expect a high return until their work is known.
How will adding a middleman effect your sales or return from those sales?

2. You are NOT looking for a sales person.

The role of an agent is to help collectors select works they'll pay for.
Don't over-dramatize the business of helping the buyer buy.
Agents should ask questions to see if a prospect meets any of these criteria.

Buyers are:
People who look at paintings and get something from the experience.
So arrange for the buyer to spend time with the painting (NOT paintings).

People who have money to buy paintings.
Don't waste time on the rest – they will want to monopolize your time.

People who like to own things they like to look at (collector).
All collectors are at least one painting away from completing their collection.

People who like to display things they own and have a place to do so.
Don't waste time on the rest – they will want to monopolize your time.

People who want to be admired for things they own and collect.
Their collection is their art as it communicates about them.

People who are probably well educated.
Their collection could be an aspect of their on-going education.
People whose parents valued and/or collected paintings etc.
Children often inherit collections and the drive as well.

People who support other arts or who read books and own them.
Also people who understand that good paintings have monetary value.
Middle-aged to elderly with established careers or comfortably retired.

People will NOT buy if:
They're starving, poor, and generally have no money.
They don't like what you do, your agent, you, or your price.
They like everything you show them.
They say they just love art.
Their wife or husband does all the art buying (after a presentation).
They're other artists.
They're members of P&C or other school parent groups.
They're politicians.
Ex-buyers who are experiencing changed circumstances.
But - people do change - sometimes!

An agent can try these tests?
Do they want to look at the painting or hear you talk (should look)?
When they are looking do they really see the work or talk (can't do both)?
When looking, are they reminded of a relative who paints (should not be)?
How long does the prospect spend with a work (speed readers don't buy)?
Give a prospect the work and see how it is handled (like delicate porcelain)?
Ask the prospect to take it closer to the natural light.
Tell the prospect to lean the work against the wall and step back for a look.
How was it placed down (gently)?

The prospect should treat the work as if it is a car bomb.

No-one knows what is "good".
EXCEPT the buyer!
Buyers spend money and have a reason for doing so.
They then become one of your best salesmen.
They have the right reasons for other buyers (you don't).

Buyers will be a salesperson to prove they haven't made a mistake.
They encourage others to buy.
Buyers can be trusted.
They know more people who buy your work the more valuable it is for them.
As prices rise this investment becomes real.
Then they are seen as smarter and thus even more influential.

Which means you and your agent will do things most artists do not do!
You make the artworks (product) and you create the studio (factory)
You and your agent do the photography, cataloguing, publicity, and selling.
You collect money and write financial reports an accountant can understand.
You and your agent plan your future, new directions, new areas to sell, etc.

People who buy can provide a good living and an excellent way of life.
Buyers like to meet the artist.
But this should be **AFTER** they've bought not before.
Otherwise they're in a compromised situation and won't talk freely.
Not about the work, why they like it, don't like it, nor their opinion.
Play the ace (meet the artist) after they've bought (so they buy again).

An agent is better than you doing ALL this and so worth paying.
BUT you probably can't afford one just **YET**.
An agent has a vital role in gaining recognition, money, travel opportunity etc.
The best agent is one you have trained.

3. An agent is a solution to your problems.

Most artists consider their job is to produce artworks.
Once a painting is completed it's time to get started on the next one.
The question of selling the works created hardly arises.
It's assumed that happens if the work is of a suitable standard and location.

Many artists think people fall in love with their work and want to buy it.
They are about the only ones who'll fall in love with their artworks regularly.
BUT they're not even buyers so having an agent is a great idea.
If the right artist and agent are linked, there are considerable benefits.
They can do all the things you do not want to do, or feel incapable of doing.

Yes, lots of artists would love to have an agent.
Then all they'd have to do is paint and the sales would come rolling in.

You assume an agent knows the market and where to get best prices.
They have contacts with outlets and a familiarity with marketing methods.
Including the market for framed art for rent and corporate purchases.
They know an image needs of publishing companies and specialist galleries.
Exposure to a wider public than would otherwise be the case.
Your work is introduced to non-local, interstate and international markets.
The purchasers become familiar with one agent.
This is preferred to negotiating one off deals with a range of artists.

The main value of having an agent is they save you time.
But, they **DO** cost money.
An inexperienced artist wants a financial return they haven't been able to get.

However the gallery or agent has its own problems.
If they can't sell your works they'll be looking for another job too.
They favour artists who are established, high priced, and make them money.
They must do this for there is really no choice.

You have to put your business hat on.
Making money is the key - failure to make money mean out of business.
Art professionals (agents, gallery) need to make money from you.
If they can sell enough, or prices are high enough they might be interested.
Your main thrust has to be how they can make money by selling your art.
Solve their problem and they'll solve yours!

So how can an agent make money by selling your art?
How you can help them do this and how much it might actually be?

The money means an agent is likely to be a service for the best artists.
Not the majority, just as it is in sport and elsewhere.
That's why they're hard to find because they are probably not looking for you.

Galleries are artists' agents and often do an excellent job, most don't.
They're easier to find than an agent and probably a better starting point.
Provided the gallery knows what to do.

The main reason someone will sell your work is they think they can.
They want to sell enough of them to make money and stay in business.
They might be interested in selling now or working with you in the future.
If they sell enough so the effort is worthwhile there's a long-term relationship.

You won't abandon your artistic integrity with a commercial approach.
That finished when you completed the painting.
You adopt a professional approach, which you must to pursue an art career.
If you can prove you and your work is marketable, your chances improve.

Read:
'What they didn't teach you at Harvard Business School' by Mark
McCormack.

4. Here's one way to find an agent!

Search through art magazines.
Look though anything from Decor to International Artist.
Study art, architecture, decorator to art business magazines.
Avoid how to art magazines and art review magazines.

Focus on trade magazines particularly if focused on selling to galleries.
In trade magazines, art dealers' ads impress galleries with their artist stable.
You can find art dealers who wholesale their art to galleries of all levels.
Occasionally an art agent will have an ad.

Develop your own skill at reading these ads.
Develop an ability to handle the phone/email contact with the dealer or agent.
You need work that compels their interest and they know will sell.
They do **NOT** take artwork on consignment but buy and resell.
It's a price that they keep secret from the artist.

Because they buy your art they put their money on the line.
They must have a confidence your artworks will sell to their clients.
They must also have confidence that you'll produce more art of equal quality.
If they buy a first painting from you which sells in four days, they'll want more.
You **MUST** be able to produce new works in a timely manner.
If they buy a work and it takes six months to sell they will not order more.

Best magazines are behind the counter at galleries and picture framers.
You have to steal them if you are not very good friends with the proprietor.
Galleries that sell to the public do not read art review magazines.
All they read are the magazines that sell to galleries.

Another approach is to hang around a gallery every day for a month.
This approach could also work at a picture framer who sells framed works.
Eventually a sales person with artworks and prints calls there.
Wait for the person to leave and introduce yourself to them.
Have a few works in your car to show.
There is much less wasted time if the proprietor provides an introduction.

Another approach is to hang around a couple of galleries.
Best if they have no interest in your work but you get on well with them staff.
Maybe you work there occasionally.

Steal some business cards and make copies with your name on them.
Use the cards to attend art trade conventions, where no artists are allowed.

Best if a proprietor provides cards and introduction to the convention.
Load your car with a stack of paintings and attend the closest convention.

Many gallery owners, picture framers and their staff attend.
There will be art wholesalers and agents with art for gallery owners to buy.
Talk to the most promising of these people (have works like yours).
Walk interested agents to your car to view your paintings that's all it takes.

5. What is your ideal agent like?

It's desirable that your agent has an accounting or legal background.
They will be negotiating and/or dealing in financial matters.
Knowledge of those professions is more useful than an art background.
But they only need enough legal or accounting to be effective agent for you.
Same goes for the art background!
In fact a person with an art background may NOT make the best agent.
Particularly if they have NO commercial background (public gallery, teacher).

Someone can learn these things as they go (at your expense).
Your husband, wife, best friend or similar person could do it.
They care about you, and your art, and want to see you successful.
They would like to help you and share in your success.

A spouse is easily the best prospect.
That's because they care about you and your art.
It provides them with an opportunity to be an important part of your world.
The main training is so they understand how you'll both be successful.
Tell them you'll set goals and rules.
Explain things step by step so they understand how you are both successful.

A better chance of a good relationship if an agent learns with you.
Someone who cares about you, loves your work, and wants to help is best.
If they have a financial or legal background that would be great.
BUT they'll learn those things anyway, so it's not essential.

But if no-one who lives with you will do it.
Then find someone you know who will which could be a friend or relative.
But caring about you and your art is not really negotiable.

Do you know anyone like that?
Do they fit the above description?
Do they need the money (better if they do)?

Will they do what you tell them?
They must, because that's the beginning of how they will learn what to do.
Otherwise this won't work as they likely think they already know what to do?
A problem for someone who is already an agent or who wants to be!

If they are willing to do what you tell them, they could be excellent.
That demonstrates a willingness to learn.
They need a computer to be in contact with clients, galleries, printers, etc.

That allows you to train your own agent.
They are responsible to you for non-artistic parts of your career you delegate.
An agent can do things you do not have the time to do.

BUT your agent is in business and so should be registered.
This can mean different things in different countries.
In Australia for example it would mean registered for GST (a tax).
Otherwise your commission cannot be claimed as tax deductible.

If you can't really find anyone – then you just have to do it yourself!
But you must distance yourself from your work (as if by another artist)
This allows collectors to be comfortable but it might be hard to achieve.
But you'll also need self-management.
How do you organize your life around this commitment?

Your art is your career and your life.
To maximize opportunities and make the money you need to keep doing it?
Commitment to your art means a lifestyle that takes you in the right direction.

Don't set the bar too low.
You should make serious progress towards whatever goals you aspire to.
Your development program is right, support systems in place and suitable.
There is no need to make a public declaration as that only adds pressure.
BUT the desire to reach those targets should be very strong.

6. Can you train someone to work for you?

YOU will be their employer.
You will need to know what they are doing and make decisions if necessary.
This is NOT the same as finding an agent to whom you supply works!

Your agent will learn what to do by doing.
They'll learn by marketing and selling your work for a probationary period.
No money made for you = continued probationary period.

You learn gradually and teach your agent the same way.
Don't try to do everything from the start.
If you do that it will no longer work!

You offer whatever financial arrangement you consider to be reasonable.
For a probationary period (6 - 12 months) it's reasonable not to pay anything.
That's because they are learning.
You are taking the risk that they'll learn well.
They'll take your proposal if they think it's OK.
They should be grateful for the opportunity.
Otherwise you negotiate or you both go in different directions.

But following that period they'll need to make money (like you do).
That comes from your sales and of other artists they then handle as well.
They also add components to your career that you do not have time to do.
These could be prints, selling copyright, art hiring and Christmas promotions.

In the probationary period you may do much of the work yourself.
The advantage of this is you'll understand what an agent can do for you.
You'll also know whether they are worth paying, whatever you want to pay.
Without an agent you'll have to do it yourself anyway!
There is **NO** way you can avoid the things you might want an agent to do.
Often that will be hard work, so in the end you'll want to escape from all that.

If you are really successful you'll need an agent to have time to paint.
Then you'll want, and be able to afford, your own agent.
The question of acquiring an agent becomes one of when rather than if.
An agent has a vital role in gaining recognition, money, travel opportunities.
As mentioned previously you are **NOT** primarily looking for a 'sales person'!

7. More money = better work?

How much should you pay?
A chief executive's pay has no relationship to how well a company performs.
In other words the money paid has no effect on results!
It's also true in most other areas of business.

If it's not money that motivates people to work effectively, what does?
For an answer we can look at the other end of the business spectrum.
The one-man or woman business, and those run by a married couple as well.
Galleries, framing businesses and a myriad of other places are like this.

Typically these people work very long hours for little money.
Usually less than any employees they may have.
They do all the things a big business does with many less resources.
Yet they keep going against what seems to outsiders, daunting odds.
They don't give up unless absolutely forced to like professional artists!

A key element is there's a dream.
They look for the day when the big wheat cheque rolls in again.
Or the business is sold for a big profit and the couple retires to live in leisure.
Or the business is franchised and is on the way to being the next McDonalds.
This belief has people doing things others consider beyond the call of duty.

Also the small businessperson can make and act on decisions.
That's a very powerful motivating force.
Ability to be your own boss is a major attraction to start your own business.
Artists are like this as you spend a great deal of time and effort on a career.
But it is your choice - you don't have to do it to please someone else!
People seek satisfaction from what they do and it's worth more than money.
It's what motivates the best executives as well as the small businessperson.
If there's satisfaction from an activity there is more energy than for money.

But it's also this attitude that keeps many artists poor!
Satisfaction is great, so business, profession, or career is run as a hobby.
If you believe you have a career, or profession **THEN** money is a measure.
It's not the motivation, that's your desire to follow your dream.

Money says something on how well you've followed the dream though.
It also makes achieving your dream more feasible.
It's unlikely a better income for an artist will lead to better work by that artist.

You are just like the executives.
BUT it will lead to a better lifestyle (just like the executives again).
You can live in a garret in poverty or the lifestyle you want - your choice.
But either way your work will remain of much the same standard.

A bigger income for an agent will not lead to better work either.
They are just like the executives too.
BUT you **WILL** get higher quality effort if you foster the dream your agent has.
If there is a suitable payoff, then you are investing time and money.
They're no longer costs but elements integral to an effective personal agent.
You also receive the benefits that flow from this arrangement.
This compounds as various elements of agent activity blend and are added.

Does a limited budget keeps you from the help you need to succeed?
Decide whether the benefits to you outweigh the cost of the solution?
The value of an agent is not just judged by the fee paid or their expenses.
It's also determined by what you get and how useful that is too.
If the balance is right then what you pay is an investment.

But it does cost money having an agent, even initially.
You won't really earn anything from the arrangement for quite some time.
Eventually you'll wonder how you did without one.
You'll have higher prices and cover the fee as well as earning more yourself.

The problem is at the start!
You must decide what you pay during training.
When will the training be completed and what you pay after that.

Payment whilst you train the agent.
During training people are not usually paid the same as when qualified.
Sometimes they earn nothing for they attend university or are apprentices.
In these circumstances they actually pay to learn their profession!

A monthly retainer + commission on money actually received.
But received as a result of their efforts.
This seems quite fair.
The retainer need not be great but it demonstrates a commitment by you.

When does the training period end?
This might be after a certain time span.
Six months is a minimum, 12 months a likely maximum but possibly 2 years.

It might be after certain things have been done.
The agent sets up, and you've had, your first exhibition as a consequence.
It might be after a certain income level is reached as a result of their activity.
Let's say she has developed $50,000 gross worth of new business for you.
It could be a combination of all of the above.
Whatever arrangement is agreed might be varied after the training ends.

How you pay a prospective agent is up to you but they work for you.
ALL money should be paid to you from the client (gallery, artist, purchaser).
Then you pay the agent according to your agreed arrangements.
Payment could be on a retainer basis.
As suggested so much a month and a % bonus income earned for you.

Following training there should be continuing income streams for you.
Then a commission only arrangement might be worth considering.
That way the agent stays on the ball.
If unsure discuss payment and come to a mutually acceptable arrangement.

After the training period concludes, they may represent other artists.
BUT keep in mind they are **STILL** working for you.
That means **ALL** money should be paid to you direct from the other artists.
Pay the agent according to agreed arrangements, different in this situation.
From this arrangement the agent can develop their own income.
But you have developed an additional income stream as well!

Your agent is paid by other artists who are their clients.
They pay more than you because they are working for you.

You both share this extra income.
Your share is less than hers (she is doing the work).
As this agency arrangement grows so does your status.
You have a strong bargaining position with galleries too.
That's due to the other artists associated with your agent.

You might consider multiple agents.
Once you have trained one, it is easier to train another.
You might consider having a different agent in major cities or regional areas.
This depends how active your first agent is and distance between centres.
A multiple agent arrangement is like a number of galleries in different areas,
Particularly when you realize that a good gallery acts as an agent anyway.
Financial arrangements should reflect a lesser influence on your career.
Possibly a commission only fee might be appropriate.

You will also need to discuss expenses.
She will need to be reimbursed for any reasonable or approved expenses.
You will need to pay these too.

8. A commission base for your agent.

Agents on commission know their future is based on repeat business.
If they don't look after their clients, they'll not return and ask for more works.
So clients actually receive more attention and 'customer service'.
If the agent knows they receive compensation for what they sell the client.
An agent will stop eating lunch to take care of a client who just arrived.
They'd make sure that when the client returns to pick up their art purchase.
The new frame is approved before work is taken home.
They'll even deliver personally to someone's home if necessary.

It is rare a non-commission agent will provide this level of attention.
It's not fair that people are paid the same with different levels of performance.
Will a top performer to be satisfied if paid the same as a lazy associate?

Can you control agent behavior on a commission based incentive plan?
What makes you think you can control them if they are not on commission?
Either way you have to manage them!!

Here are a few of the elements of a smart compensation plan:
All agents are on the same basic plan
Compensation is on performance of measured elements not just sales.
The percentage increases as key performance numbers are met.
Your career 'nets' more profit with over performing agents.

You'll need a contract or an agreement.
Your agent will handle many matters only previously dealt with by you.
A contract should set out the nature of arrangements with your agent.
It takes into account your needs and expectations as well as the agents.

Offering a contract facilitates clearing up potential misunderstandings.
It may be difficult, but it's still better than trying to sort things out much later.
Often a problem is not a problem, but needs explaining or expressing clearly.
If there is something they don't like, they can argue to delete, or amend.
You can accept these things too, if everything else is satisfactory.
So can your prospective agent.

Often artists feel uncomfortable about written contracts.
Consequently many agreements are of a handshake variety.
This is fine if you both really understand what is required and expected.
AND the agent understands what you expect of them as well but, do you?

Do you really understand an agent's expectations?
On the first occasion you meet a prospective agent or enter into negotiations.
Have a reasonable discussion about what they expect of you.
If a gallery is an agent, the discussion should be before you show paintings.

What needs to be covered with a gallery as an agent?
Include the obvious ones, their commission rate and retainer.
Clarify how you are paid following a sale and **WHEN** they are paid (monthly).
What will happen when a client is paying off a work?
At an exhibition will there be any extra payments and if so what will they be?
Who is responsible for pricing (they may assume it's their role)?
What sort of support will they want from you?
Do not assume this will be OK, as in many cases it's not!

Anything you are uncertain about, you should ask about.
Assuming is a process that often leads to later problems.
You should be certain you know what the agent will do for you.
It is really dumb not to ask dumb questions!
Do they really understand your expectations?
Ensure you have a reasonable discussion about your expectations of them.

An important aspect is finance.
Your agent is working for you thus any money earned should be paid to you.
Then you pay your agent according to your contractual agreement.
How soon will they be paid following a sale?
What will happen when a client is paying off a work?
When you have an exhibition will there be extra bonuses?
If so what will they be, and how much will they be.
How should they plan to sell your works if they are not in an exhibition?
Just ask about anything you want to know!

The agent should be certain they know what you'll do for them.
They'll need a Job Description that you both are happy with.
What sort of support will they want from you?
This might be written material or your presence at functions they arrange.
What is their view on you selling your own works or using a gallery agent?
Do not assume this will be OK it needs discussing.

How do they plan to sell works if not in an exhibition or at a gallery?
Initially a prospective agent may not have answers, but eventually they will.
Anything you are uncertain about, you should discuss.
Assuming is a process that often leads to later problems.
You should be certain you know what the agent will do for you.

Misunderstandings do happen!
Sometimes there is deception but agents are as honest as artists.
Most friction between artist and an agent comes through misunderstanding.
Generally they are about answers to the questions suggested above.
Don't assume an agent means what you think.
Ask them what is meant exactly, even if you think you know.
Have regular scheduled meetings.

What records do you need?
You could have computerized stack sheets, as many artists do.
However a simple system is to have a delivery book, bought at a newsagent.
List artworks to be left, with price, name of the gallery or agent and date left.
Write other special conditions, and the gallery owner or agent signs the page.

Issue them with the original and a carbon copy in a delivery book.
They may also give you a consignment note.
This is similar document, but issued by the gallery or agent to an artist.
There should be exchanged signed documents to accompany leaving artwork.
This applies even if your agent is your spouse.

What basic information is needed?
Most agreements need names and addresses, as well as signature and date.
At least for the parties making the agreement, as well as from witnesses.
The timeframe of the agreement, details of any penalties that apply.
Loss or damage to stock, or failure to meet deadlines, could be included.
These can be expressed in simple English (or whatever your language is).
It will be legal though.

The most important documentation is your own agent's job description.
That's an outline of what he/she will do.

Much of this will be adopted and adapted as part of learning what to do.

WHERE NEXT:

**BUT being a professional artist is NOW harder than it ever was.
These books are on earning money from a professional art career.**

Gallery Co-Operation
http://www.amazon.com/dp/B087637FFW

Selling Strategies
http://www.amazon.com/dp/B0882JH3WN

Copyright
http://www.amazon.com/dp/B0892HWYTV

Make Exhibitions Work
http://www.amazon.com/dp/B0882MFPGX

Art Hiring
http://www.amazon.com/dp/B0884JWR2S

Your Website
http://www.amazon.com/dp/B08846SWQP

Courses and Workshops
http://www.amazon.com/dp/B0884B51JB

Selling Prints
http://www.amazon.com/dp/B08846SWQW

Retirement
http://www.amazon.com/dp/B0884D9TBP

Art School
http://www.amazon.com/dp/B08849FV59

**BUT being a professional artist is NOW harder than it ever was.
This book is the last on earning real money from an art career.**

TAKE THE PLUNGE and Consider a Gallery.
http://www.amazon.com/dp/B0874JF964
Hardback
http://www.amazon.com/dp/B09GQRB34T

NOT NOW:

Perhaps one of these books could interest you then?

Write about your own memories.
YOU could publish them – like I did!
http://www.amazon.com/dp/B087DWKPTP

A simple way to start developing creativity.
If you are a parent, teacher or someone who meets a group regularly?
http://www.amazon.com/dp/B088T1KFQZ

This is the way most people start to become an artist!
http://www.amazon.com/dp/B088Y1DPL6

Some more of my memories.
http://www.amazon.com/dp/B088Y4RPL9

SEND TO:

Know anyone interested in chocolate recipes? Send them a link then.
http://www.amazon.com/dp/B0882HK9Q9

Know anyone interested in THIS book?
http://www.amazon.com/dp/B08847Y9KS

www.ingramcontent.com/pod-product-compliance
Lightning Source LLC
Chambersburg PA
CBHW030533220526
45463CB00007B/2820